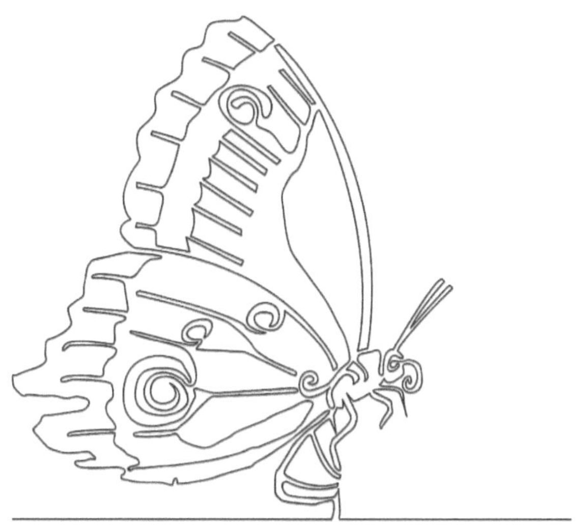

Butterflies & Black Girls

poetry-to-read-aloud

by

Raedorah Con'ett Stewart

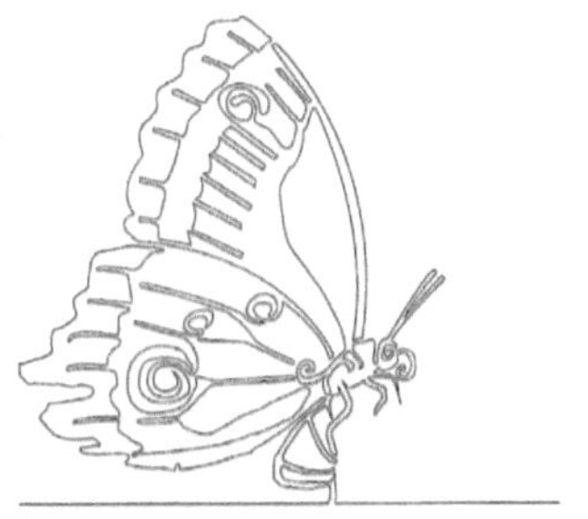

Butterflies & Black Girls

Raedorah Con'ett Stewart

Acknowledgments

Myself.
I am proud of myself for being healed enough to publish finally
poetry as a collection that I have written, performed,
and laid out in book form since 1980. It's 2024.

I am less afraid.
And, if I die before I wake, I want Black Girls,
even those we Old Ladies tend inside to read these poems aloud
and not wait 44 years to transcribe their lives in words.

My daughter (née son).
Her poetry and audacity to live keep me living.
Less afraid.

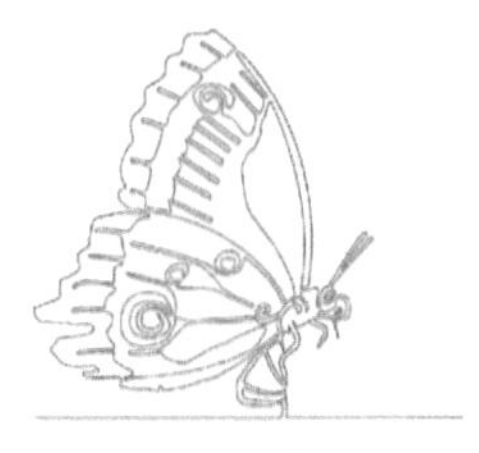

Preface

Butterflies & Black Girls: poetry-to-read-aloud is excerpted from my unpublished collection of poems I have written over 44 years, ***Colored Womyn's Commentary***

I write poetry to keep myself company. To talk to whomever listens about real pain and anticipated pleasure. To think through my next move. To work out a bad mistake. To cry when tears won't fall. To laugh at every opportunity. To lament and groan. To celebrate and remember. To leave a legacy of words to my son/sons/daughter/daughters; especially the ones I didn't birth but who still need to know.

I perform poetry to sing my black girl songs and tell my colored womyn's story. To make the record. To set the record straight. To give voice, loud and clear, to those who'd instead I keep silent.

I learned to love/listen to/make my own colored womyn's commentary by eavesdropping when grown women gathered at the kitchen table instead of playing outside with the rest of the children; by reading grown women's words before I got grown/gone from my mama's house; by daring to live/love like a grown colored woman who expects to live forever despite efforts to kill me/my/spirit/mind.

Some of the words are autobiographical, indeed. Still, most are what Audre Lorde would name *biomythological:* my voice/lens for recording what happens to/around me. True and valid and necessary.

Butterflies & Black Girls is a whole-body experience meant to be read aloud, cried over, laughed about, danced to, and shared with others to entertain, encourage, and educate.

Be sure to get my permission to publish or record for performance. Better still, invite me to read/perform/compose for your next blackgirl/coloredwomyn's gathering.

Raedorah Con'ett

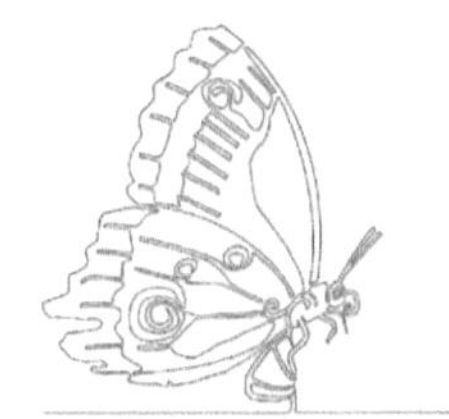

Contents

Lil'Girl

Birthright

©1981

June 4, 1960, 4:54 a.m. I was born
a Black babe

8 lbs, 10 ozs, 22 ins long
and a wail that shook the walls of the delivery room

I was announcing my arrival
the one to be often imitated, never duplicated

I was christened
Raedorah Con'ett Stewart
(with an 'e' and an 'h' and an 'apostrophe)

I grew up in the bowel of a Houston ghetto
too tall, too skinny, too sassy

The height let me pass as an older woman
the skinny got me lots of hand-me-downs
and the sassy matured into intelligence

June 4, 1981, I became
a Black woman!

A Diamond in the Rough

©1984

I catch you stealing glances at me now
The look on your face asks, "How?"
For what you see before your eyes
That is to you a great surprise
Is a lady, really strutting her stuff.

A little girl is who you remember
Growing a bit between January and December
With nappy hair, acne, and ashen knees
Imposing peer pressure or aiming to please
Sparkling now, I was then, a diamond in the rough.

Butterflies & Black Girls

Reflections of butterflies
reveal souls of Black girls

We who have evolved
from being wrapped up so tight in negativism
isolated by prejudice and
made ignorant to that we would change

The burdens of this land
tried to make us weak
tried to break us down
tried to harness our speech

Drained what some thought
was our last ounce of pride
but from our natural reserves
came strength though
many had suffered and died

Oh, but we were just lying dormant
Our souls did survive
And like the butterfly of springtime
We beautiful Black girls arrive.

Color Me Old

when I get old
I'm gonna wear the funkiest shades of
Purples, Reds, and Greens
all at the same time
accented with Yellows all the time

the kids next door will call me crazy
the good church folk will say I'm touched
the human services aides will sigh in disbelief
all at the same time
`cause I probably will be all the time

you see when I get old

Purples will be the colors of my dreams
long after cataracts
have veiled my eyes
expect them, the doctor said
big mama and mama had them, you know

Reds will be the fires, as I remembered igniting them
long after my steps are shorter
and arthritis swells my knees
with seductive dances, skintight pants,
and razor-sharp charm
then I had you know

Greens will be my passion for life
long after my voice begins to waiver
quiet my thoughts will be, and
senility may make me forget the date you know
but it will be the

Yellows that will really catch their eye
as I feel the warmth of a sunrise
and see the beauty of a sunset
long after they sit around
coffeehouses, campfires conferencerooms
and kitchentables reading my poetry
reminiscent of my spirit
remembering that when I got old
I did wear the funkiest shades of
Purples, Reds, and Greens all at the same time
accented with Yellows all the time
actually, long before I got old.

At About 10

And the sweet potato
stain my hands, reminding me
of the pain of peeling off the undesirable
to get to the naturally sweet meat
nature wrapped inside.

I remember oh so vividly
managing to peel just the skin away
`cause Mama would kill me
if I was in one of my trifling days
and wasted good potato
from one that was twice the size of
 one of my hands and managed not to
slice my left arm in two!

By the time I'd peeled enough
maybe 1/2 dozen or so
I looked at the stains
I wring my hands in pain
 but I did remember how sweet
those candied yams would be!

Twisted Sister

©4/02

Mama's middle child
twisted sister, they called her

All b'cuz they couldn't
and most times, just wouldn't

hear the drums
I danced to til I broke out into a funky sweat
hear the drums
I thought to ever contemplate before committing
hear the drums
I marched to with long-legged strides and swaying hips
hear the drums
I talked to laughing, crying sometimes out loud
hear the drums
I played on my private self with fingers in the dark
hear the drums
I loved to while waiting for that lover of a lifetime
hear the drums
I smiled to from my soul
calming babies   wooing womyn
leaving them wondering

Mama's middle child
twisted sister, they called her/me

they couldn't, they wouldn't
hear my drums.

Tired Little Girls

©1996

Little girls who look tired
grow up to be tired-looking women
who had seen
too much
too soon
through little girls' eyes.

Mama's Girl

The Prerequisite of Womanhood

©1982

Up from the Congo
flowing down the Nile
born of the fertile soil of the Motherland
The Motherland land of Black mothers
land of the first Black mother

She bore the seed to replenish the land
to keep the soil fertile
she bore herself a baby girl
the prerequisite of womanhood

And she watched that seed grow to be
as lithe as limber as Black as she
and she watched that seed taken from its soil
into a land called America

There she became
just another pickaninny on some anonymous
plantation in Dixie
From dawn to dusk in the cotton fields
she did what she had to do to live
"yes mam'ing" and "no sir'ing"
she watched her men beaten and
her daughters raped
she cried a river of tears

but she believed in God
and she believed in a better day
that's why she bore her baby again

The baby of segregation
oh, you remember the times when all nigras
had to enter from the back
sit at the back and
stay in the back...
The baby of integration
when it took the National Guard in Little Rock
the sit-ins at the soda fountains and
the death of Dr. Martin Luther King, Jr.

The baby of Black Power
"Dig my foot high `fro
my psychedelic logo
my authentic dashiki
Black Power, Black Power,
Black Power's in me!"

But just like her mother and her mother before
she knew that she, too, must bear the seed
to replenish the land
to keep the soil fertile
She bore herself a baby girl
and that, baby, was Me!

Me, deal with my African identity?
My slavery ancestry?
My segregated, integrated, and Black indemnity?
Who, Me?
the one who is educated, refined, and rides
not only on the front of the bus
but first class on 747's
Who, Me?

Oh, you're damned right. I'll deal with it
'cause it is Me
My mama from the Motherland
gave Me my rhythms
My mama from the Dixieland
gave Me my strengths and
My mama of this Americanland
gave Me my freedom
to live to do to be that what I am
A Black Woman.

And one day
I'll bear the seed to replenish the land
to keep the soil fertile
I'll bear me a baby girl
the prerequisite of womanhood.

Don't You Know Who Yo' Mama Is?

©1993

Taking coffee with your sugar again?
Gotta high, and you're trying to keep
Pimping flesh and favors just for a place to sleep?
Whose child are you anyway?

Talking show trash done got your brain?
You go on it to tell it all
About these no-good brothers
Evidently, lacking balls?
What would your mama say?

Taking the easy way out of your pain?
Nerve pills are liars that take
Even more of your sanity
And sets up your wake.
How did she make it through such a day?

Baby, don't you know who yo' mama is?
The giver of life! A good man's wife! A survivor of strife!

Today, say, "I can be more like my mama."

My Mother's Friend

©1993
(Other Women)

She reminds me of my mother's friend
Lou Joyce really does
Nappy natural with just enough gray
to know that she was a stone-cold fox in the '60s

She reminds me of my mother's friend
Juanita really does
Weeping mother always feeling somebody else's pain
most often of children she bore 30-some-odd years ago

She reminds me of my mother's friend
B. Ruth really does
Wise woman beyond her years from keeping secrets
of life's experiences –
good, bad, a lesson learned in all

She reminds me of my mother's friend
Dee really does
Loud laughter finding funny in a pet playing
or retelling of a good time full of original joy

She reminds me of my mother's friend
Cora really does
Quiet smile more perfect than a picture
that tells of inner peace that comes with knowing God

She reminds me of my mother's friend
Gladys really does
Busy body but hurting nobody
always looking out for somebody else or their child

She reminds me of my mother's friend
Really she does
You know the one who loves, cares, concerns, comforts
You know, the ones so much like my mother.

When Mama Was God

When Mama was God
She made miracles happen
In the middle of a Houston ghetto
The center of my universe, indeed.

She walked on water
In three-inch heels, matching bag
With us five kids in her footsteps.

She taught us to fear not
Night lightning, thunderstorms
Hard work, new things, good success.

When Mama was God
She created not one but two
Fancy Easter dresses and sewed
Lace on my socks to match.

She hollered for me from the porch
Compelling me to come out, come out
From all my favorite hiding places.

She held me close with strong hands
So close that I would inhale
Warm, fleshy bosom heat for air.

When Mama was God
She stood her ground with white folk
Those blue-eyed devils of pure evil
Of the '60s… '80s… this new millennium.
She laid hands on us/me
So the cops wouldn't and trifling men couldn't
Healing bad attitudes and broken hearts.

She made a dollar holler
On the occasions of more month than money
Without robbing anyone of anything.

When Mama was God
She blessed two fish and five loaves
Or was that govm't cheese
And canned mystery meat.

She kept an open-door policy
Always meant that somebody else
Would be sleeping on the living room floor.

She prayed for us and others
We eavesdropped, listening for our name
Knowing that no weapon formed against us
would prosper.

When Mama was God.

"Girl, you just like your mama,"
somebody said one day
when I was feeling a whole lot like God.

My Mother's Smell

©1983

My earliest and most profound memory
of my mother
is the pungent smell of jungle Gardenia.
Found at the 5¢ & 10¢,
 it smelled like Sak's Fifth Avenue   on her
whereas nobody else could stand to wear it
 and had little tolerance for smelling it
but admitted that it didn't smell nicer
on anyone else they knew.

I associated the scent
with mother's playfulness and laughter
Warmed up between the fleshiness of her bosom
my being engulfed between her body heat
and the intoxicating effect of jungle Gardenia
made for what is now total recollection
of security and serenity and being loved.
It also acknowledged
the threat of an impending punishment
 (either/both applied with intense severity)
for some known or unknown childhood crime
committed just today or in yesterdays

I go home sometimes now
just to smell my mother
and her jungle Gardenia
I want to let her know that's why I came
I want to let her know that I love her

but it remains unsaid, and I sneak
concentrated whiffs of jungle Gardenia straight from the bottle

I don't think she'd understand
a grown woman
wanting her to hold her tight and
resurge the intensity of the memory.

Even if that woman is one, she created?

Our House Was Way Too Big

Our house was way too big for you to be
hungry for a meal
homeless for a month
helpless for a minute

In our house, Sunday meals very often became
two fish and five loaves
Twin beds slept two
next to dozens of pallets
Needs known became needs met
all in the same breath

In our house, there was plenty daily bread
in hugs and in hamhocks
twice as many pillows and blankets as bed
and always somebody ready
to care and to comfort

In our house, there was always enough to go around.

Mama's Old Brown Couch

©1995

More than decoration, it was an invitation
Mama's old brown couch
to family, friends, and next of kin
it welcomed our sitting down
to hold conversations across generations
mama's old brown couch.

More than mere structure, it was a place to mature
Mama's old brown couch
whether in body, mind, or spirit
it was a preparing place to discover one's self
or somebody else
mama's old brown couch.

Doing its best at holding tears and calming fears
Mama's old brown couch
is in the family forever, barely aging at all
an invitation still today for whoever needs a stay
on Mama's old brown couch.

Its Sunday Afternoon

©1993

It's Sunday afternoon
and my home smells like my mother's house
when she was raising us
Right

After church, we styled three blocks home
all dressed up in homemade clothes
skipping and humming some church song
And right

At the door, we could smell what was cooking
what was put on this morning just before we knelt to pray
turn down low so nothing scorches just
Right

The smell was a handshake to our many years of dinner guests
and a hug to all of us

And right
now my home smells just like my mother's house.

My Mama, the Grandmother

©1994
(for Mama & JJ)

When my mother became a grandmother
to my son, especially
I admit to often wondering if she'd do it effectively.

Would she slow down enough
To walk him in the mall
to talk his baby languages
and hear him when he call?

Would she somehow find the time
to bake him a special pie
to toss the ball until he caught it
and count the stars in the sky?

Would she let him run to her
for conquest over dark fears
for building up and showing off
and comfort his big boy tears?

I wondered only for a little while
actually, more for like a minute
'cause every time she even looks his way
I can see her love for him in it!

Quilted Arms

©2002

A perfect place
reviving the soul with history
reliving the history with labor

A perfect place
for you to remember who your people are
for you to privately regret how you acted out

A perfect place
knowing here there will be no judgment
knowing here is sanctuary as long as you need

A perfect place
for you to cry just because it hurts so bad
for you to celebrate good success and love to last

A perfect place
when another lecture is too much
when silent understanding is better

A perfect place.
Quilted arms.

Quilted Legacy

©2002

It was Big Mama not Mama
who taught me to quilt

to take scraps of well-worn leftovers discards
to tend to them sorting washing trimming
to make them useful again

with the pattern in her head labor in her hands
the cloth would have another chance
to be beautiful
refashioned to function

as a quiet place for healing
a warm place for new babies
a great place to take a
Sunday afternoon nap

as a still place to hear ancestors
as an intimate space for loving
a great place to spend the day
daydreaming

as a wall hanging telling history
as a bed covering of exquisite beauty
a great way to learn to be
and make friends

It was Big Mama
who taught me how to quilt.

My Sister Sings

©1995

My sister sings like I dance
and it is more than just art
Her song and my dance
are the beats of our hearts
our words when we speak
our tears when we cry
our aura and mystique
our epitaph, should we die.
My sister sings like I dance.

Sister Sistuh

©1993
(Terry)

Milk sisters come from the womb of the same mother.
Kin by lineage
Blood sisters come by the cross of Christ Jesus
Kin by heritage
Sister Sistuhs come by way of being women.
Kin by calling out, 'Hey girl!'
Kin by combing out nappy hair
Kin by cooking up good food
Kin by checking on your kids
Kin by catching your slack #' watching
Kin, by comforting your broken heart

We missed being milk sisters
It just wasn't the plan
We are eternally blood sisters
Always in His hand
We became sister sistuhs
Because we loved ourselves so much
that we wanted another one of us to
 join our celebration of life and
all the other stuff sister sistuhs do!

My Daddy's People

©1997

I don't usually count my daddy's people
among the folk who made me

grow up to be as smart as I am
as wise as I am becoming
as loving as I long to be

when he left, they did, too, and
neither had been around much before, anyway

but occasionally
I am prompted to think about my daddy's people
and then only able to remember a few of their faces
having forgotten a lot of their names
and no sense at all of who they
married, divorced, sired, or now live with

but occasionally
a genogram to chart relationship
or the lack thereof
 a medical history for a proper diagnosis
or my son would inquire
'Mama, do you have a daddy?"

Big Girl

I've Been Mixed Like Cornbread

©1988

I've been mixed like cornbread
And I'm not that instant brand
Measured out, not by metered cup
But with the skills of a knowing hand.

The flour of my soul
And the meal of my mind
Rises with the heat
And the salts of time.
I've been mixed like cornbread.

Two eggs for self-identity
A dash of sugar to make me sweet
Add the day-old fatback drippings
And this cornbread's complete.

I tickle your taste buds to a salivary greeting
After exactly 23 minutes at 375
Top me off with the real fresh butter
You welcome our meeting as I now arrive.
I've been mixed like cornbread.

So, serve me up. I'm a favorite dish
With the likes of collard greens, buttermilk, or fish
I've been mixed like cornbread
And I'm here to complement
Your first life course.

Code Switching

©1996

Looking black
talking black
sounding white
to be HEARD, I cannot relax my tongue

Thinking black
writing black
walking white
to be SEEN, I gotta go to the resources

Acting black
acting black
acting white
to GET what you got to do
to get what I NEED to.

Bookshelf Groans

©1995

The bookshelf groans
carrying the weight of
who I was when I read that
feminist, womanist, anti almost everything
who I am while reading this
cooking, parenting, divorcing
who I am becoming when I read the other
theology, psychology, philosophy
The bookshelf groans
it is time to get another one.

Laundry Rooms

Why is it that laundry rooms
often house a lot of
dirt in the corners
dust on the rafters
int on the floor and
crud in the vents

Is it to welcome the dirt brought in?
And does it grieve
when the laundry leaves clean?

Black Girls Tell Big Lies

©1986-88

I get the feeling she really wouldn't have minded
you know
being killed would have been just another lie
of course
But the truth is that she wasn't
but did it for the Cause
And now,
I sometimes question whether have we lost the cause of '66
 `cause in '86, we are lost
or are we really still digging the truths
from Angela's lies?

Are you ready yet
for more Black girls to tell big lies?

Purple has always been my favorite color
so when Alice Walker lied in The Color Purple
I was able to see the fact beyond the film and the fiasco
Celie Nettie, your love was
colored a purple of pain and uncertainty
making it glow an inseparable hue
Celie Shug, the joy of discovering a love of self
gave your purple a shade of empowerment
Oh sistuh, we're two of a kind, sho' nuff

And there are so many more finding solace in
God's purples in a blackened world
colored by the brothers'
colorblindedness to appreciate us

And don't bother blaming me this time, brother
for being the way you are
I have no one to blame when I grow colorless

Neither did our sistah Pat Cowan
playing a part in purple when a brother   *her loverman*
bludgeoned her   *to death*
with her child   *their 4-year-old son*
taking notes

Girl, you gotta be lying!
Uh uhnn
though most folks are inclined to think so.

Black girls tell big lies
laced with truths so real
you got no choice but to believe us.

New Products

©1981

There it was, in the corner window of the department store

NEW PRODUCTS

Fashion Fair Cosmetics had arrived to
make me a more magnificent mama!

Skin tone: bronze glow
Chocolate chip contour...

Look out Nefertitti, Cleopatra and Sheba
Make way for me!

Almond-shaped eyes with potential,
A dash of green, black, gold, and plum...

Honey, these big browns are on the loose!

Full Black Lips:
(Or just plain old big nigga lips is ok with me)
outline, then fill in with bright red or hot pink
(Understand now, my rich coloring could take these colors well)

First glance   a shock
Then I like it.

Cause I realize since I am so beautiful anyway,
I have a choice.

The Artist and the Poet

©1992
(Carla)

There was once an Artist:
A creator of shape and form
With magic in her hands like the sun.

And like the rainbow after the rain
She produced colors from the plain.
A dash of indigo, chartreuse and red
A life was made from a canvas so dead.

There was once a Poet:
A creator of rhythm and rhyme
With magic in her words, that kept time.

And like the ticking of the clock
Her words, the poems, never stop.
Some endings may rhyme, and others not end
But the essence of her poems will not be forgotten.

Though they knew not of the other
They thought quite the same.
They both had an idea
But they each a different name.

To the artist, it was painting
To the poet, it was rhyme.
But they both created women,
"Here's to the women on our minds."

When I Had a Baby

©1996

When I had a baby, I got fat
Got not just a pretty baby
but a lot more than that

I got breasts upon which heads could lay
and while making love now would sway

I got a little belly muscles stretched and flabby places
wouldn't dream of sweating it off
only covering up with lacies

I even got some butt now no more carpenter's delight
but rather more to roll with upon our bed at night

I got thighs holding up these hairy legs
and hiding treasures for which you'll surely beg

When I had a baby, I got more than that and
I'll never miss a meal nor bemoan my being fat

Cause what I got is now all mine
Breast, belly, bulges, and behind!

Mama, Will You Many Me?

Mama, will you marry me
my little boy employed
inspired, I'm sure, by happy times often enjoyed

Each other's company was always well-spent
and it didn't take much for me to know what he meant

By asking such a question
was his man love imitation l
earned from his parent's kissing and cartoon inspiration

And so for now, until he's 21
I accept my reign as queen of his life
Until such time, he inquires of another
Will you marry me and be my wife.

Mama, Pretend

©1997
(JJ)

45

Mama pretend
these are my children and
I am the daddy and
you are the granny, and
we are going to the park and
don't forget to give all of us
pretend vitamins and
real love.

Great Big Smiles

©6/02
(JJ)

Great big smiles on little boy faces
Make you forget your heart was broken
by his Y chromosome
Make you want ice cream in winter
wearing woolen mittens
Make you have to run through water sprinklers
fully clothed
Make you need to play an endless game
of Monopoly on a rainy day
Make you laugh like you did
when you used to be a kid
Make you pray
that his joy remains full and complete
Make you fear for him the days ahead
when a harsh reality hits him
Make you kiss him when he's asleep
and doesn't respond to your affection.
Great big smiles on little boy faces
The gift that keeps on giving long after he's grown and gone.

Grieving with a Childless Mother

©1994
(Other Mothers)

The mothers whose babies were aborted
are sometimes haunted when another baby cries
when another mother wipes their weeping eyes
when a toddler stands up from a crawl
and she catches him before he could fall
Go ahead, it's all right to grieve for yourself.

The mothers whose babies miscarried
oftentimes wake up through the night
can't put her finger on it, but something's not right
then she remembers the life she never held and tears in her eyes,
but from her soul begins to well
Go ahead, it's all right to grieve for yourself.

The mothers whose womb had to be removed spends
time taking care of another mother's blessing
rocking her to sleep and mindlessly caressing
knowing breasts never to swell and let down
hiding behind the laugh covering a frown
Go ahead, it's all right to grieve for yourself.

The mothers for years without a father
make time to listen to our motherly woes
of wiping runny noses and ironing matching clothes
and is always available to lend a hand to babysit
all the while hoping to be fulfilled by this one wish
Go ahead, it's all right to grieve for yourself.

Why the life I carried I now hold in my hands
Is something I won't even pretend to understand

I have no explanation why some mothers get the chance
And others resign themselves to a mourner's dance.
But, go ahead, it's all right to grieve for yourself.
I'll just grieve alongside you.

Celebrate Your Labor

©2002

I wasn't there didn't know you when
you delivered your baby boy

but know that I heard you holler when
you told your story sobbing
tears burning holes in my heart

I wasn't there didn't know you when
you delivered your baby boy

but know that I hollar still when
wondering where the rest of your womenfolk were
while you were lying there fighting to live and give life

Out of the Attic

I remember a little girl
laying *awake* at night
staring at the attic door
imagining my worst fright.

What if? What would happen if
the ghosts beyond the door
would knock to enter, turn the knob
come into the present to *explore?*

My big brown eyes welled up with tears.

I hold my breath
my palms then sweat
my heart beats fast
I'm just not ready yet!

For the secrets beyond the door
that whisper even louder still
with all my might, I've been taught to "shush" them
but they beckon me *against my will.*

Cute Old Women

©1995

Cute old women
wear red hair
wear blue hair
wear eyebrows brown, gray
and Maybelline black.

Cute old women
wear polyester
wear plastics
wear plaids, checks
and flowers on the same outfit.

Cute old women
never fade in spirit
never faint in soul
never finish living.